AI Bookkeeping, Accounting & Tax Records

How AI Keeps Perfect Financial Documentation

By Joe Corre

Published by Live Stronger Faster

This book is for educational and informational purposes only. The author and publisher are not engaged in rendering legal, financial, tax, or other professional advice. Readers should consult a qualified professional before making any financial decisions.

First Edition

Table of Contents

Introduction

In the modern business world, bookkeeping and accounting are no longer just background tasks quietly handled by back-office staff or outsourced firms—they have become the very foundation of profitability, tax efficiency, and long-term survival. Every dollar that enters or leaves a company creates a data trail that directly determines how much tax is paid, how much cash remains available, how attractive the business appears to lenders and investors, and how exposed it is to audits and penalties. Yet for decades, companies have relied on error-prone human systems, scattered spreadsheets, delayed reconciliations, and inconsistent documentation. Artificial intelligence changes this forever. AI does not simply record transactions; it builds a living, breathing financial nervous system for a company—one that captures every movement of money, classifies it correctly, verifies it against multiple sources, and produces flawless tax-ready records in real time. This book explores how that transformation works and how businesses can use AI bookkeeping and accounting systems to create financial clarity, compliance, and competitive advantage.

Traditional bookkeeping has always been reactive. Transactions happen first, then weeks or months later someone tries to reconstruct what happened by hunting through bank statements, credit card records, invoices, and receipts. This delay creates errors, missed deductions, cash-flow surprises, and tax exposure. AI reverses this model. In an AI-powered accounting environment, financial data is captured the moment it is created. When a sale is made, an expense is incurred, a payroll transaction is processed, or a transfer occurs, AI instantly records it, assigns it to the proper account, applies the correct tax treatment, and links it to supporting documentation. Instead of working backward from chaos, the business operates forward with certainty. This is the difference between running a company in the dark and running it with full financial vision.

What makes AI bookkeeping so powerful is not just speed—it is intelligence. AI understands context. It knows the difference between a marketing expense and a capital asset, between a reimbursable travel cost and a deductible business meal, between taxable income and tax-deferred revenue. It learns patterns over time, recognizing how a business operates and automatically applying accounting rules with increasing accuracy. Unlike human bookkeepers, AI does not get tired, does not forget, and does not misclassify transactions because of workload or distraction. Every data point strengthens the system, creating an accounting engine that becomes more precise with every transaction processed. This intelligence transforms tax compliance at its core. Tax law is built on documentation. The IRS does not simply want numbers; it wants proof. AI creates that proof automatically. Every expense is tied to a receipt, every revenue entry is tied to a customer transaction, every depreciation schedule is tied to an asset purchase. When tax season arrives—or when an audit occurs—the financial story of the business is already assembled, verified, and organized. There is no frantic scrambling for records because the records already exist in a structured, digital, audit-ready format. AI bookkeeping turns compliance from a stressful event into a continuous state of readiness.

At the same time, AI accounting gives businesses something even more valuable than compliance: control. When financial data is updated in real time, business owners always know exactly where they stand. They know how much cash is available, how much is owed, how much is receivable, how much tax liability is building, and how profitable each part of the business truly is. This clarity allows smarter decisions. It allows companies to time purchases for maximum deductions, adjust payroll or contractor spending, restructure debt, or invest in growth without fear of financial blind spots. AI turns accounting into a strategic tool rather than a historical record.

For small businesses, this revolution is especially powerful. Historically, high-quality accounting systems were expensive and required teams of professionals. AI makes enterprise-level bookkeeping available to everyone. A startup, a freelancer, an online store, or a growing corporation can all access the same level of financial intelligence. This democratization of accounting creates a new kind of competition—one where financial accuracy, tax efficiency, and compliance become standard rather than rare. Businesses that adopt AI bookkeeping gain an immediate edge over those still relying on manual systems.

Another critical advantage of AI bookkeeping is fraud and error detection. AI constantly scans transactions for anomalies. It flags duplicate charges, mismatched invoices, unusual vendor activity, and patterns that indicate mistakes or misuse of funds. This protects businesses from internal theft, billing errors, and financial leaks that quietly drain profitability. In a traditional system, these problems might go unnoticed for months. In an AI system, they are detected almost immediately. Financial integrity becomes automatic.

AI also brings seamless integration across every financial platform. Bank accounts, credit cards, payment processors, payroll systems, inventory tools, expense apps, and tax software all feed into a single unified accounting brain. Instead of juggling multiple disconnected systems, businesses operate with one synchronized financial truth. This eliminates reconciliation errors, lost data, and reporting inconsistencies. Everything aligns. Everything matches. Everything is verifiable.

As businesses grow, their financial complexity increases. More customers, more vendors, more employees, more tax obligations, more regulatory requirements. AI scales effortlessly with this complexity. It does not require hiring more staff or paying more for processing—it simply processes more data. Whether a company has 100 transactions a month or 100,000, the system remains fast, accurate, and reliable. This scalability is what allows modern businesses to grow without their accounting becoming a bottleneck.

From a tax optimization perspective, AI bookkeeping is the engine that powers every strategy in this series. You cannot optimize deductions, protect profits, or defend against audits without clean, complete, and accurate records. AI provides that foundation. It ensures that depreciation schedules are correct, that payroll taxes match filings, that sales tax is calculated properly, and that financial statements reflect reality. When records are perfect, strategy becomes possible. When records are messy, even the best tax plan collapses.

This book will show you how AI accounting systems work behind the scenes, how they classify and validate data, how they integrate with tax platforms, and how they protect your business from errors and penalties. You will learn how to set up AI bookkeeping so that it becomes the silent financial guardian of your company—capturing every dollar, protecting every deduction, and maintaining constant compliance.

In the age of artificial intelligence, bookkeeping is no longer a chore. It is a strategic asset. It is the system that turns transactions into insights, compliance into confidence, and data into decisions. AI bookkeeping does not just keep records—it builds financial certainty. And in a world where tax laws grow more complex and regulators become more aggressive, that certainty is one of the most valuable assets a business can own.

Chapter 1

The AI Accounting Revolution: From Chaotic Books to Perfect Financial Control

For most of modern business history, bookkeeping has been one of the least glamorous yet most dangerous parts of running a company. It was always treated as a necessary chore—something that had to be done to satisfy the IRS, prepare financial statements, or apply for loans—but rarely as something that actively made a business stronger. Receipts were stuffed into shoeboxes, spreadsheets were copied and pasted from month to month, and accounting systems were patched together by overworked humans who were expected to somehow create perfect financial order from incomplete, delayed, and often contradictory information. This fragile model created a hidden tax on every business in the form of missed deductions, incorrect filings, cash flow surprises, and audit exposure. Artificial intelligence changes that entire equation by turning bookkeeping from a backward-looking record into a forward-looking financial command center.

AI accounting systems do not simply record transactions after the fact. They watch money move in real time. Every sale, every expense, every payroll run, every transfer, and every refund becomes a data event that is instantly captured categorized, validated, and stored. Instead of reconciling accounts at the end of the month and hoping nothing was missed, AI keeps everything in balance continuously. Bank feeds, credit card feeds, merchant processors, and accounting ledgers all stay synchronized. If a number does not match, the system flags it immediately. This creates a financial environment where errors cannot hide and problems cannot grow quietly in the background.

What makes AI so powerful is its ability to understand context. A human bookkeeper must be trained on what counts as advertising, travel, cost of goods sold, office supplies, depreciation, and dozens of other categories. AI learns these distinctions by observing behavior, transaction descriptions, vendor histories, and industry patterns. Over time, it becomes more accurate than a human ever could be. It recognizes that Facebook charges are marketing, that Amazon purchases may be inventory or office supplies depending on patterns, and that a software subscription is an operating expense rather than a capital asset. This intelligence ensures that financial statements are not only accurate but optimized for tax efficiency.

Another major shift AI introduces is continuous documentation. In the past, businesses would collect receipts and invoices sporadically, often losing them or misplacing them. AI systems automatically attach documents to transactions, pulling them from email, scanning them from phone cameras, or receiving them directly from vendors. Each expense becomes a complete record: date, amount, vendor, category, tax treatment, and proof. This creates what auditors and tax authorities value most—a clear, verifiable trail that proves every number on a tax return. AI turns documentation into a built-in function rather than a desperate afterthought.

This level of precision changes how businesses experience tax season. Instead of scrambling to reconstruct a year's worth of activity, companies using AI bookkeeping already have their books closed, reconciled, and categorized. Financial statements are ready. Depreciation schedules are updated. Payroll and sales tax records are aligned. Tax software can pull clean, structured data directly from the accounting system and generate accurate filings with minimal human intervention. The anxiety, delays, and errors that used to define tax preparation disappear because the data is already correct.

AI also brings unprecedented transparency. Business owners no longer have to wait for monthly reports to understand what is happening. They can see revenue, expenses, profit margins, tax liabilities, and cash flow in real time. This allows smarter decision-making. A company can see immediately whether it can afford to hire, invest, or expand. It can see which products or services are truly profitable. It can see when tax obligations are rising and adjust strategy before problems occur. Financial awareness becomes continuous instead of periodic.

Perhaps most importantly, AI accounting makes financial integrity automatic. Fraud, double billing, incorrect payroll, and unauthorized spending are detected by pattern-recognition algorithms that never stop watching. If something looks unusual, the system flags it. This protects businesses from both internal and external threats. Instead of trusting that nothing went wrong, companies know when something does.

AI bookkeeping also scales effortlessly. A business can go from 100 transactions a month to 100,000 without changing its accounting infrastructure. The system simply processes more data. This is crucial in the modern economy, where online sales, subscription billing, and global customers can cause transaction volumes to explode overnight. AI keeps up without missing a beat.

In this new paradigm, bookkeeping is no longer just about compliance. It becomes the backbone of profitability, risk management, and growth. Every financial decision is supported by clean, accurate, real-time data. Every tax strategy is built on a foundation of perfect records. Every audit is met with confidence rather than fear. This is the AI accounting revolution—and it is redefining what it means to run a financially healthy business.

"The Ledger That Never Slept"

When Miguel opened his digital marketing agency, he believed the hardest part would be finding clients. He was wrong. The real nightmare began six months later, when his bank balance didn't seem to match his revenue, his credit cards were maxed out, and his accountant kept asking questions he couldn't answer. He had sales coming in from Stripe, expenses going out through PayPal, contractors paid through multiple platforms, and receipts scattered across email inboxes, phones, and browser downloads. Every time tax season approached, he felt like he was standing in front of a financial crime scene trying to guess what had happened. He knew he was making money, but he had no idea where it was going.

The first audit notice came like a punch to the stomach. The IRS wasn't accusing him of fraud—but they wanted proof. Proof of expenses, proof of income, proof of deductions. Miguel spent weeks digging through old emails, downloading statements, and trying to piece together a story that made sense. His accountant warned him that missing documentation could mean penalties, interest, and lost deductions. Miguel realized that even though his business was successful on the surface, it was financially fragile underneath.

That was when a friend introduced him to an AI bookkeeping platform. Miguel was skeptical at first. He had tried accounting software before, but it always required constant manual input. This was different. Once connected, the system pulled in every bank account, every card, every payment processor, and every invoice. It didn't just import the data—it understood it. Within hours, the AI had categorized his transactions, identified missing receipts, and flagged discrepancies he didn't even know existed.

Over the next few weeks, Miguel watched something incredible happen. Every time he spent money, the AI recorded it. Every time a client paid, it appeared instantly in his dashboard. Receipts were automatically attached. Cash flow became visible. Profit became measurable. For the first time, Miguel could see his business clearly. It felt like someone had turned the lights on.

When the IRS followed up, Miguel was ready. He didn't send boxes of paperwork or messy spreadsheets. He sent structured reports, categorized expenses, and complete documentation for every deduction. The audit closed without penalties. What once felt like a looming disaster became a non-event. But the real transformation came afterward. With clean, real-time books, Miguel started making smarter decisions. He cut waste. He adjusted pricing. He planned tax payments instead of being surprised by them. His business became calmer, more predictable, and more profitable.

Miguel used to think bookkeeping was something you survived. Now he knew it was something that could protect and empower you—if it was done right. And thanks to AI, his ledger never slept again.

Chapter 2

Real-Time Financial Intelligence: How AI Sees Every Dollar the Moment It Moves

In the old accounting world, businesses were always looking backward. Financial statements reflected what happened last month, last quarter, or last year, but rarely what was happening right now. By the time a company discovered a cash-flow problem, an expense leak, or a revenue decline, the damage was already done. Artificial intelligence changes this by turning bookkeeping into a live financial radar system. Every transaction becomes a real-time data signal that allows businesses to see, analyze, and respond to financial activity as it happens, rather than after it has already created problems.

AI systems connect directly to every financial source in a business: banks, credit cards, payment processors, payroll platforms, invoicing systems, expense apps, and inventory tools. Instead of manually importing or reconciling data, the system continuously syncs everything into a unified financial model. The moment a customer pays an invoice, the AI updates revenue. The moment a bill is paid, the AI updates expenses. The moment payroll runs, the AI adjusts liabilities and cash balances. This creates a financial heartbeat that never stops, giving businesses a constantly accurate view of their financial position.

This real-time visibility transforms cash-flow management. Cash flow is the lifeblood of any business, yet it is one of the most misunderstood financial metrics. Traditional reports show how much money came in and went out, but they do not show timing, trends, or future risk. AI models cash flow dynamically. It predicts when money will arrive, when bills will be due, and when cash balances will be tight. This allows businesses to avoid overdrafts, late fees, and emergency borrowing. Instead of reacting to cash shortages, companies plan for them.

AI also provides instant profitability analysis. Every sale and every expense is assigned to products, projects, clients, or departments. This allows businesses to see exactly what is making money and what is losing it. In a traditional system, these insights might require hours of manual analysis or expensive consulting. In an AI system, they appear automatically. A business owner can see which marketing campaigns are profitable, which clients are worth keeping, and which services should be eliminated or repriced. This makes financial decision-making data-driven rather than emotional. Another powerful feature of real-time AI accounting is tax forecasting. Every transaction affects tax liability. Sales create income. Expenses create deductions. Payroll creates employment taxes. Sales tax creates obligations to the state. AI continuously calculates how each transaction changes the company's tax position. This allows businesses to know their true after-tax profitability at any moment. Instead of being shocked by a massive tax bill at the end of the year, companies see their tax exposure building in real time and can adjust spending, investments, and compensation accordingly.

Real-time financial intelligence also strengthens internal controls. AI monitors spending patterns, vendor activity, and account behavior. If something deviates from normal—an unusually large payment, a duplicate charge, or a suspicious vendor—the system flags it immediately. This protects businesses from fraud, mistakes, and financial abuse. Instead of discovering problems months later, companies catch them when they are still small and fixable.

The integration of real-time data also makes reporting effortless. Financial statements are always current. Balance sheets, income statements, and cash-flow reports update automatically. Lenders, investors, and tax professionals can access accurate data whenever needed. This eliminates the delays and errors that come from manual reporting cycles. Perhaps most importantly, real-time AI bookkeeping changes how business owners think. They stop guessing. They stop hoping. They stop being surprised. They operate with financial clarity. They know exactly where they stand and where they are headed. In a world where speed, agility, and precision determine success, this level of financial awareness becomes a competitive advantage that few companies without AI can match.

"The Dashboard That Changed Everything"

Sophia ran an online fashion brand that looked wildly successful from the outside. Social media was buzzing, orders were flowing in, and influencers were wearing her designs. But behind the scenes, Sophia lived in constant fear. Some months she had plenty of cash. Other months she struggled to pay suppliers. Her accountant sent reports weeks after the month ended, and by then the numbers were already outdated. She felt like she was driving a race car by looking only in the rearview mirror.

Everything changed the day she connected her business to an AI accounting system. At first, it was just interesting. She could see sales appearing on her dashboard the moment customers checked out. Then she saw shipping costs, ad spend, and payment processing fees flowing in real time. Slowly, a clearer picture emerged. Some of her best-selling products were barely profitable after marketing and fulfillment costs. Some of her slow-moving items were actually high-margin gems.

One afternoon, Sophia noticed something alarming. Her advertising costs had spiked dramatically in the last two hours, but sales had not increased. The AI flagged the campaign as underperforming. She paused the ads immediately. In the old system, she wouldn't have noticed for weeks. That single decision saved her thousands of dollars.

As the weeks went by, Sophia began to trust her dashboard more than her instincts. It told her when to reorder inventory, when to cut spending, and when she could afford to launch a new line. It even showed her how much tax she owed as profits grew, so she set money aside instead of being blindsided later.

For the first time, Sophia felt in control. Her business no longer felt like a chaotic gamble—it felt like a machine she could see and steer. The real-time numbers didn't just show her what was happening; they gave her the power to change what would happen next. And that made all the difference.

Chapter 3

Audit-Ready by Design: How AI Builds Perfect Tax Records Automatically

One of the greatest fears in business is not just paying taxes—it is being asked to prove them. An IRS audit is not about how much tax you paid; it is about whether you can justify every number on your return. For decades, businesses have lived with a quiet vulnerability: even when they acted honestly, their records were often incomplete, disorganized, or inconsistent. Missing receipts, misclassified expenses, or delayed reconciliations could turn a legitimate deduction into a costly penalty. Artificial intelligence changes this by creating audit-ready records as a natural byproduct of everyday operations. With AI bookkeeping, compliance is no longer something you prepare for later—it is something that is built in from the beginning.

AI accounting systems create a continuous chain of evidence for every transaction. When money moves, the system captures the amount, date, vendor, account, and purpose. It then attaches documentation automatically, pulling invoices from email, receipts from scanning apps, and confirmations from vendors. This means every financial entry is not just a number in a ledger—it is a fully supported financial event.

Auditors care about evidence, and AI creates that evidence in real time without relying on memory, filing cabinets, or human discipline.

This structure is what turns chaotic business activity into a coherent financial story. A traditional audit often becomes a painful reconstruction process, where accountants try to piece together what happened months or years ago. AI eliminates this by preserving the story as it unfolds. Every revenue stream, expense category, asset purchase, and payroll run is recorded with context. The system knows why money was spent, not just that it was spent. That context is what makes records defensible.

Another powerful feature of AI bookkeeping is consistency. One of the biggest red flags in an audit is inconsistent classification. If a company treats the same type of expense differently across months or years, it invites scrutiny. AI applies rules uniformly. Once it learns how a business classifies advertising, travel, inventory, or software, it applies those rules the same way every time. This creates clean, predictable financial patterns that stand up to examination.

AI also manages depreciation and asset tracking with extraordinary precision. Instead of manually tracking equipment, vehicles, and software purchases, AI assigns each asset a digital life cycle. It knows when it was bought, how it should be depreciated, and how much value remains. This prevents over- or under-depreciation, both of which can trigger audits or tax adjustments. Every asset becomes part of a transparent, verifiable tax strategy.

When tax returns are generated, AI pulls directly from these clean records. There is no need to estimate, guess, or reconstruct. The numbers match the books because the books were always correct. This dramatically reduces audit risk, because discrepancies between tax filings and accounting records are one of the most common triggers for investigation.

Perhaps the most profound impact of AI audit-ready systems is psychological. Business owners no longer live with a background fear that something is wrong in their books. They know that if an auditor ever asks, the answer is already there. Confidence replaces anxiety. Compliance becomes automatic rather than stressful.

In a world where tax authorities are becoming more data-driven and more aggressive, AI bookkeeping is not a luxury—it is a shield. It turns every transaction into a documented truth. And when your financial truth is clear, consistent, and complete, audits lose their power.

"The Day the Auditor Smiled"

Ethan owned a growing logistics company that moved freight across three states. On paper, it was thriving. In reality, his bookkeeping was a mess. Different drivers submitted expenses in different ways. Fuel receipts were missing. Equipment purchases were tracked in one system and depreciation in another. When the audit notice arrived, Ethan felt like the ground had disappeared beneath him.

His accountant told him the truth: they could try to reconstruct the records, but it would be painful and risky. That was when Ethan decided to implement an AI bookkeeping system, even though the audit was already underway. He figured he had nothing to lose.

The system connected to his bank accounts, fuel cards, payroll, and invoicing software. It began organizing years of data in days. Transactions that once looked like random numbers now had meaning. Every fuel purchase was matched to a truck. Every repair was linked to a piece of equipment. Every driver payment was categorized correctly. Missing receipts were requested automatically.

When the auditor arrived, Ethan didn't bring boxes of paper. He brought a digital portal. The auditor could click any number and see the documentation behind it. There were no contradictions. No gaps. No confusion.

Something unexpected happened. The auditor smiled.

The audit closed with minimal adjustments. No penalties. No accusations. Just confirmation that the records were solid.

Ethan realized something powerful: his business had been profitable before, but now it was protected. The AI system didn't just keep books—it told the truth about his company in a way that no one could challenge. And that truth gave him a kind of freedom he had never felt before.

Chapter 4

From Transactions to Truth: How AI Turns Raw Data into Financial Clarity

Every business produces enormous amounts of financial data, but data alone does not create understanding. Bank feeds, invoices, payroll records, receipts, subscriptions, and transfers generate thousands of numbers that mean nothing unless they are structured, interpreted, and connected. Traditional bookkeeping systems collect data but rarely transform it into insight. Artificial intelligence changes this by converting raw transactions into financial truth—clear, consistent, and decision-ready information that reflects the real state of a business at any moment in time.

At the heart of AI bookkeeping is data normalization. Every financial source speaks a slightly different language. Banks describe transactions one way, credit cards another, payment processors another, and vendors another. AI translates all of these inputs into a unified accounting language. It strips away inconsistent descriptions, identifies vendors correctly, and standardizes transaction types so that financial records are coherent rather than fragmented. This alone eliminates one of the biggest sources of accounting confusion: mismatched data that never quite lines up.

Once transactions are normalized, AI applies intelligent classification. Instead of blindly assigning categories, AI evaluates patterns, vendor behavior, historical usage, and business context. It understands that the same vendor might represent different expense types depending on frequency, timing, and description. Over time, the system becomes deeply familiar with the financial personality of the business. This means fewer corrections, fewer reclassifications, and more accurate financial statements. Accuracy compounds as the system learns.

AI then layers verification on top of classification. It cross-checks transactions against receipts, invoices, contracts, and payment confirmations. If something does not align, it flags the discrepancy. This continuous verification prevents errors from becoming permanent. It also ensures that financial reports reflect reality, not assumptions. In traditional systems, errors often persist for months because no one notices them. In AI systems, errors are detected almost immediately.

With clean, verified data in place, AI generates clarity. Income statements stop being confusing summaries and become precise reflections of profitability. Balance sheets stop being mysterious snapshots and become accurate representations of financial health. Cash-flow statements stop being abstract concepts and become practical tools for planning. Business owners no longer wonder whether their numbers are right—they know they are.

This clarity extends beyond compliance into strategy. AI accounting systems allow businesses to see trends forming before they become problems. Rising costs, declining margins, inefficient spending, and seasonal patterns become visible. Decisions are no longer based on intuition alone. They are supported by data that has been continuously refined, validated, and contextualized.

Another critical benefit of AI-driven clarity is communication. Clean financial records make it easier to work with accountants, tax professionals, lenders, investors, and partners. Everyone sees the same numbers, structured the same way, supported by the same documentation. This reduces friction, misunderstandings, and delays. Financial conversations become productive instead of painful.

Clarity also creates confidence. Business owners who understand their numbers operate differently. They invest more wisely. They negotiate better. They plan further ahead. They are less reactive and more intentional. AI bookkeeping does not just improve records—it improves leadership.

In an increasingly complex tax and regulatory environment, clarity is protection. When financial data is clean and truthful, compliance becomes natural. Reporting becomes accurate. Audits become manageable. Growth becomes sustainable. AI turns financial chaos into order and order into advantage.

"The Numbers Finally Made Sense"

Daniel had always trusted his instincts. He built his consulting firm on experience, relationships, and intuition. But as the business grew, his instincts started failing him. Some months felt profitable but ended with empty bank accounts. Other months looked slow but somehow paid the bills. His accountant sent reports, but Daniel didn't understand them. The numbers felt abstract, disconnected from reality.

When Daniel adopted an AI bookkeeping system, he expected automation. What he didn't expect was understanding. Slowly, the numbers began to tell a story. Revenue streams separated themselves clearly. Expenses revealed patterns. He saw which clients were profitable and which quietly drained time and money. He saw subscriptions he forgot he had. He saw inefficiencies he had normalized.

One afternoon, Daniel noticed a trend the AI highlighted: a steady increase in operating costs that didn't correlate with growth. He dug deeper and discovered redundant software tools and unnecessary contractors. Cutting them improved his margins immediately. For the first time, decisions felt obvious instead of stressful.

As tax season approached, Daniel felt calm. The records were clean. The reports were clear. The numbers made sense. He realized that his business hadn't changed—his visibility had. AI hadn't replaced his instincts; it had sharpened them.

Daniel no longer feared his financial reports. He welcomed them. They told him the truth. And with that truth, he finally felt in control.

Chapter 5

Closing the Books Without Stress: How AI Automates Accuracy, Reconciliation, and Trust

For generations, the phrase "closing the books" has carried a sense of dread for business owners and accountants alike. Month-end and year-end closings were synonymous with late nights, frantic reconciliations, missing transactions, unexplained discrepancies, and uncomfortable conversations about numbers that didn't quite add up. The process was slow, manual, and vulnerable to human error. Artificial intelligence fundamentally changes this experience by transforming the close from a painful event into a continuous, nearly invisible process. With AI, the books are never truly "open" or "closed"—they are always accurate.

At the core of AI-driven closings is continuous reconciliation. Traditional accounting systems wait until the end of the month to reconcile bank statements, credit cards, and ledgers. By that point, errors have multiplied and memories have faded. AI systems reconcile transactions as they occur. Every deposit, withdrawal, transfer, and charge is matched to its corresponding ledger entry in real time. If a transaction cannot be matched, the system flags it immediately, while the context is still fresh and the solution is easy to find. This prevents small discrepancies from becoming major problems.

AI also eliminates one of the most common sources of closing delays: timing mismatches. Payments may clear days after they are initiated. Deposits may batch differently across platforms. Manual systems struggle with these timing issues, often creating temporary imbalances that confuse reports. AI understands these patterns. It recognizes pending transactions, accruals, and settlements, ensuring that financial statements reflect economic reality rather than bank timing quirks. This produces cleaner, more accurate reports without manual intervention.

Another powerful advantage of AI-assisted closings is rule-based consistency. AI applies the same accounting rules every time, without fatigue or judgment drift. Accruals, deferrals, revenue recognition, and expense matching follow predefined logic that remains stable across months and years. This consistency strengthens financial credibility. When numbers behave predictably, stakeholders trust them. When they don't, confidence erodes. AI restores that trust by making financial behavior reliable. As the system learns a business's rhythms, it begins to anticipate closing needs. It knows which transactions usually arrive late, which accounts need periodic adjustments, and which reconciliations require special attention. Instead of reacting at the end of the month, AI prepares continuously. By the time a formal close occurs, most of the work is already done. What once took weeks can now take hours—or minutes.

This automation has a profound impact on year-end tax preparation. Because monthly closings are clean and consistent, year-end adjustments are minimal. There is no scramble to fix twelve months of mistakes. Depreciation schedules are up to date. Payroll accounts reconcile correctly. Sales tax liabilities align with filings. The year closes smoothly because it was managed correctly all along.

AI also creates transparency in the closing process itself. Business owners and financial teams can see exactly what has been reconciled, what is pending, and what requires attention. There are no black boxes or mysterious adjustments. Every number has an explanation. This visibility reduces stress and improves collaboration between internal teams and external advisors.

Beyond efficiency, automated closings improve decision-making. When financial statements are always current, businesses no longer delay decisions while waiting for reports. They act with confidence, knowing the numbers are accurate. This agility is a competitive advantage in fast-moving markets.

In the AI era, closing the books is no longer an ordeal. It is a confirmation. A confirmation that the financial story has been told correctly, consistently, and completely. AI turns closing from a crisis into a formality—and that shift changes how businesses experience accounting forever.

"The Quietest Month-End Ever"

Karen had built her manufacturing business with discipline and grit, but month-end was always chaos. Every closing cycle felt like a crisis. Her accounting team stayed late, reconciled accounts manually, and argued over numbers that never quite matched. Karen dreaded board meetings because she never fully trusted the reports she presented. There was always a lingering fear that something was wrong beneath the surface.

When Karen approved the switch to an AI-driven accounting system, her motivation was simple: survival. She couldn't keep running a business that held its breath every month. At first, the transition felt subtle. Transactions flowed in automatically. Reconciliations happened quietly in the background. Alerts replaced emergencies.

Then month-end arrived.

Karen waited for the familiar tension. It never came. The system showed that most accounts were already reconciled. A handful of exceptions were flagged days earlier and resolved quickly. Financial statements were ready almost immediately. No overtime. No panic. No last-minute fixes.

The following months were the same. Clean closes. Accurate numbers. Calm meetings. Karen noticed something unexpected: her leadership team started asking better questions. Instead of debating the numbers, they discussed strategy. Growth. Investment. Efficiency.

Karen realized that the chaos had never been inevitable—it had been a symptom of broken systems. With AI handling reconciliation and accuracy, her business felt lighter. More stable. More professional.

For the first time in years, month-end passed quietly. And that silence told her everything she needed to know.

Chapter 6

Scaling Without Chaos: How AI Accounting Supports Growth, Complexity, and Control

Growth is often portrayed as the ultimate goal of business, but in reality, growth is one of the most dangerous phases a company can experience. As revenue increases, transactions multiply, compliance requirements expand, payroll grows, and reporting obligations become more complex. Many businesses do not fail because they lack customers; they fail because their financial systems collapse under the weight of expansion. Artificial intelligence changes this dynamic by allowing companies to scale without losing control. AI accounting systems are designed not just to handle growth, but to thrive in it.

In a traditional accounting environment, scaling requires proportional increases in labor, oversight, and manual processes. More transactions mean more reconciliations. More employees mean more payroll complexity. More locations or sales channels mean more reporting requirements. This linear relationship between growth and administrative burden creates friction that slows expansion and increases risk. AI breaks this relationship. Once implemented, AI systems handle increasing volume without increasing complexity. Ten transactions or ten thousand are processed with the same accuracy, speed, and consistency.

One of the most powerful aspects of AI accounting at scale is its ability to manage complexity invisibly. As businesses expand into new markets, launch new products, or adopt new revenue models, financial structures become layered and interconnected. AI maps these layers automatically. It understands how different revenue streams interact, how expenses should be allocated, and how financial data should roll up into consolidated reports. This prevents fragmentation, where different parts of the business operate with different financial truths.

AI also supports scalable compliance. Growth often triggers new tax obligations, reporting thresholds, and regulatory oversight. Manual systems struggle to keep up with these changes, increasing the risk of noncompliance. AI continuously monitors regulatory requirements and applies the appropriate rules as the business evolves. Sales tax thresholds, payroll obligations, and reporting standards are tracked automatically. This ensures that compliance keeps pace with growth instead of lagging behind it. Another critical benefit of AI accounting at scale is predictive insight. Growth creates uncertainty. Cash flow becomes harder to predict. Costs fluctuate. Investment decisions carry greater risk. AI uses historical data and real-time inputs to model future scenarios. It shows how growth will impact cash reserves, tax liabilities, and profitability before decisions are made. This allows businesses to grow intentionally rather than reactively.

AI also strengthens internal alignment during growth. As teams expand, financial understanding often becomes siloed. Different departments operate with partial information, leading to inefficiency and conflict. AI creates a single source of financial truth that everyone can access. This transparency improves collaboration, accountability, and decision-making across the organization.

Perhaps most importantly, AI preserves financial discipline during periods of success. Many businesses become careless when revenue increases, allowing costs to rise unchecked and controls to weaken. AI does not get complacent. It applies the same scrutiny at every stage, ensuring that growth does not erode profitability or integrity.

Scaling with AI accounting is not about growing faster at any cost. It is about growing smarter, safer, and more sustainably. AI provides the structure that allows ambition to expand without chaos. It ensures that as businesses become bigger, their financial foundation becomes stronger—not weaker.

"The Company That Outgrew Its Old Numbers"

When Victor started his software company, he knew every number by heart. He could tell you daily revenue, monthly expenses, and cash on hand without checking a report. His business was simple then—one product, one payment processor, a small remote team. Accounting was manageable, even informal. Growth came quickly, and with it came complexity. New pricing tiers. International customers. Contractors in multiple countries. Multiple bank accounts. Multiple tax obligations. Victor didn't notice the danger at first because the money kept coming in.

The first sign of trouble wasn't a loss—it was confusion. Victor's dashboards no longer agreed with each other. His bank balance didn't match his revenue reports. His accountant asked questions Victor couldn't answer. Profitability felt real, but it was impossible to measure accurately. Growth had outpaced visibility.

As the company doubled and then tripled in size, the cracks widened. Payroll became stressful. Taxes became unpredictable. Forecasts became guesses. Victor realized that the system that had supported his startup could not support his company anymore. He wasn't running a small business—he was running an organization, and it needed a different kind of financial brain.

The transition to AI accounting was uncomfortable at first. Victor felt exposed. The system connected everything—every account, every transaction, every obligation. For the first time the numbers told a story that wasn't filtered by optimism. Some products were underperforming. Some expansion decisions had been premature. Some costs had grown silently.

But clarity brought relief. The AI didn't judge—it organized. It showed Victor exactly how growth had changed the company's financial structure. It mapped revenue streams. It allocated costs accurately. It reconciled accounts continuously. Slowly, order replaced chaos.

As months passed, something remarkable happened. Growth stopped feeling dangerous. Victor could launch new features and enter new markets with confidence because he could see the impact immediately. Cash flow stabilized. Tax planning became proactive instead of reactive. The company became calmer even as it became larger.

One evening, Victor reviewed a consolidated report showing performance across all regions. The numbers made sense. They aligned. They told the truth. He realized that the problem had never been growth itself—it had been trying to grow with tools designed for something smaller.

The company hadn't just outgrown its old accounting system. It had outgrown uncertainty. And with AI guiding its financial core, Victor knew that whatever came next, the numbers would keep up.

Chapter 7

The Single Source of Financial Truth: How AI Eliminates Conflicting Numbers Forever

One of the most damaging problems in business accounting is not outright error, but contradiction. When different reports show different numbers, confidence collapses. Revenue from one dashboard doesn't match the bank balance. Payroll totals don't align with expense reports. Tax filings don't perfectly reconcile with accounting statements. Each system may be partially correct, yet none of them agree. This fragmentation creates doubt, delays decisions, and increases compliance risk. Artificial intelligence resolves this problem by establishing a single, authoritative source of financial truth—one continuously updated, validated, and reconciled system that every stakeholder can trust.

AI accounting systems are designed to eliminate duplication and contradiction at the data level. Instead of maintaining separate records across tools that must later be reconciled, AI ingests all financial activity into one unified model. Bank transactions, invoices, payments, expenses, payroll, assets, and liabilities are linked to a shared data structure. When a number changes in one place, it changes everywhere. There are no competing versions of reality. There is one truth.

This unified structure transforms reporting. Financial statements generated from an AI system are not assembled manually—they are derived directly from the same validated data that powers daily operations. This ensures that income statements, balance sheets, cash-flow reports, and tax schedules are always aligned. When lenders, investors, accountants, and regulators review the numbers, they see consistency instead of confusion. Trust increases because clarity replaces contradiction.

The single source of truth also improves accountability. When numbers are fragmented, responsibility becomes blurred. Teams argue about which report is correct instead of addressing underlying issues. AI removes this ambiguity. Because every transaction is traceable and every report is derived from the same source, discrepancies are resolved quickly and objectively. Financial discussions become productive instead of defensive.

AI further strengthens truth by enforcing rules consistently across time. Accounting policies, categorization logic, and compliance standards are applied uniformly, regardless of volume or complexity. This prevents drift, where classifications change subtly over time due to human inconsistency. Stability in financial logic creates stability in reporting.

For tax purposes, this unified truth is invaluable. Tax filings rely on the integrity of underlying records. When those records are fragmented, audits become dangerous. AI ensures that tax returns reflect the same data used for internal reporting. There are no surprises, no unexplained differences, no gaps between accounting and compliance.

Ultimately, a single source of truth changes how businesses operate. Leaders stop questioning their numbers and start using them. Decisions are made faster. Planning becomes more accurate. Confidence replaces hesitation. AI doesn't just reconcile data—it reconciles reality.

"The Meeting Where No One Argued About the Numbers"

The first time it happened, Olivia thought something was wrong.

She sat at the long conference table surrounded by her executive team, waiting for the usual debate to begin. This meeting—monthly financial review—had always followed the same script. Someone would point out a discrepancy. Someone else would defend their spreadsheet. Finance would blame timing. Operations would blame accounting. Sales would insist their numbers were right. The meeting would end with frustration and no real decisions.

But this time, silence filled the room.

The report on the screen showed revenue, expenses, margins, cash flow, and tax reserves. Everything lined up. No footnotes. No caveats. No "we'll have to double-check that." Olivia looked around, expecting someone to object.

No one did.

Just a year earlier, Olivia's company had been drowning in data and starving for truth. They had grown fast—too fast for their systems. Sales used one dashboard. Finance used another. Payroll lived somewhere else entirely. The numbers never agreed, and Olivia never fully trusted any of them. Every major decision felt like a gamble.

The breaking point came during a failed expansion. The numbers had suggested the company could afford it. The bank balance had said otherwise. Olivia realized that growth hadn't failed—visibility had. She authorized the shift to an AI-driven accounting system, knowing it would expose uncomfortable truths.

And it did. The first weeks were unsettling. The AI connected everything. It revealed inconsistencies they had normalized. It showed how timing differences, duplicate records, and manual adjustments had created multiple versions of reality. It didn't accuse. It corrected. Slowly, the numbers began to converge.

Departments resisted at first. Sales didn't like losing their custom reports. Operations didn't like the new transparency. Finance worried about being replaced. But as weeks turned into months, something changed. Meetings became shorter. Reports stopped contradicting each other. Decisions started sticking.

Now, sitting in that quiet room, Olivia realized what had changed wasn't just the data—it was trust. No one argued because there was nothing to argue about. The numbers were the numbers.

The discussion moved forward. They talked strategy. Investment. Hiring. Risk. Growth. The meeting ended early.

As Olivia walked back to her office, she smiled. For the first time in her career, the hardest part of leadership—deciding what was real—had been solved. The truth was no longer something they searched for. It was something they shared.

Chapter 8

From Compliance to Confidence: How AI Transforms Financial Anxiety into Strategic Power

For most business owners, accounting has never been a source of confidence—it has been a source of quiet fear. Fear of missed deductions. Fear of incorrect filings. Fear of audits. Fear that something is wrong beneath the surface and will eventually surface at the worst possible moment. Even profitable businesses often operate under this psychological burden, carrying uncertainty about whether their financial systems can withstand scrutiny. Artificial intelligence changes not only the mechanics of bookkeeping, but the emotional experience of running a business. It replaces anxiety with assurance and compliance with confidence.

Traditional accounting systems demand vigilance. Business owners must constantly wonder whether transactions were recorded correctly, whether documents were saved, whether categories were applied consistently, and whether reports truly reflect reality. This constant mental load distracts leaders from growth and innovation. AI removes this burden by making correctness the default state rather than the result of effort.

When financial systems validate themselves continuously, trust replaces worry.

AI builds confidence by closing gaps before they become risks. It does not wait for tax season or audits to expose weaknesses. It identifies missing documentation, misclassifications, timing issues, and anomalies as they occur. This proactive behavior prevents small problems from becoming large liabilities. Instead of reacting defensively, businesses operate with foresight.

Another key transformation AI enables is narrative clarity. Financial data is not just numbers—it is a story about how a business operates. When that story is fragmented or inconsistent, confidence erodes. AI ensures that every report tells the same story, supported by the same facts. This coherence allows business owners to speak about their finances with certainty, whether to investors, lenders, tax professionals, or regulators.

AI also changes the role of financial advisors. When records are clean and reliable, accountants and tax professionals move from firefighting to strategy. Conversations shift from fixing errors to optimizing outcomes. This elevates the entire financial ecosystem around the business, creating smarter decisions and better results.

Perhaps the most profound impact of AI bookkeeping is internal. Business owners who trust their numbers think differently. They plan further ahead. They take calculated risks. They invest with intention. They stop hesitating. Financial confidence becomes strategic power.

In an increasingly complex regulatory environment, confidence is not arrogance—it is preparedness. AI does not eliminate responsibility; it supports it. It ensures that businesses meet their obligations consistently and transparently. Compliance becomes routine rather than stressful.

Ultimately, AI transforms accounting from a source of fear into a foundation of strength. When businesses know their financial truth, they stop worrying about being exposed and start focusing on what they can build next.

"The Year Nothing Went Wrong"

The strangest thing about the year was not how much money the company made—it was how little panic there was.

Rachel noticed it in February. Normally, by then, she would already be stressed. Tax documents would be trickling in. Reports would be half-finished. Her accountant would be sending emails with subject lines that made her stomach tighten. But this year felt different. Quiet. Too quiet.

Rachel ran a professional services firm with multiple revenue streams, contractors in different states, and clients on recurring contracts. For years, success had felt fragile. Every win came with the lingering fear that something had been recorded incorrectly. She remembered nights lying awake, replaying expenses in her head, wondering if receipts were saved, wondering if she would be ready when questions came.

The transition to AI bookkeeping had happened the year before, out of exhaustion more than optimism. Rachel didn't want magic—she wanted stability. At first, the system felt almost invasive. It connected everything. It asked questions. It flagged issues she didn't know existed. It forced clarity.

That clarity had been uncomfortable. The AI exposed inefficiencies Rachel had tolerated for years. Subscriptions she forgot about. Contractors who were overutilized. Expenses that had quietly crept upward. But once exposed, those issues became manageable. Fixable.

By spring, Rachel realized something remarkable: her accountant had stopped asking frantic questions. Instead, they talked strategy. They discussed timing. They discussed future scenarios. Tax planning became calm, almost boring. Then summer came. A former employee challenged an expense reimbursement. The documentation was ready. No scrambling. No reconstruction. The issue resolved quickly.

In the fall, a lender requested updated financials. Rachel sent them the same reports she used internally. No adjustments. No disclaimers. The loan was approved faster than expected.

By December, Rachel looked back on the year with disbelief. No surprises. No crises. No emergency calls. The business had grown steadily, calmly, predictably.

One evening, as she reviewed year-end reports, Rachel felt something unfamiliar: peace. The numbers made sense. They matched. They told the truth. She realized that for the first time in her career, success didn't feel fragile.

Nothing had gone wrong that year—not because problems didn't exist, but because they were handled before they became threats. AI hadn't made her business perfect. It had made it resilient.

Rachel closed her laptop and smiled. For the first time, the future didn't feel risky. It felt ready.

Chapter 9

Future-Proofing the Financial Core: How AI Prepares Businesses for Regulation, Risk, and What Comes Next

The final responsibility of any serious accounting system is not just to explain the past or manage the present, but to protect the future. Businesses do not operate in static environments. Tax laws evolve, reporting standards tighten, enforcement tools become more sophisticated, and regulators gain access to increasingly powerful data-matching technologies. What passed unnoticed ten years ago can now trigger automated scrutiny in seconds. Artificial intelligence prepares businesses for this reality by building accounting systems that are adaptive, resilient, and designed for a future of continuous oversight rather than periodic review.

Traditional bookkeeping systems are fragile because they depend on fixed rules, static workflows, and human intervention to adapt to change. When regulations shift, systems lag behind. Updates come late. Mistakes occur in the transition period. AI accounting systems operate differently. They are designed to absorb change. When tax thresholds shift, filing requirements expand, or documentation standards evolve, AI adjusts classification logic, reporting structures, and compliance workflows automatically. This adaptability allows businesses to remain compliant without scrambling to reconfigure systems or retrain staff under pressure.

AI also future-proofs businesses by creating records that are not merely compliant today, but defensible tomorrow. As audits become increasingly digital, authorities rely less on individual documents and more on patterns, consistency, and cross-platform verification. AI excels at this level of scrutiny. It produces records that are internally consistent, chronologically complete, and mathematically aligned across systems. When data is analyzed years later, it still holds up. This long-term integrity is one of AI's most overlooked advantages.

Risk management is another area where AI fundamentally alters outcomes. Financial risk is rarely caused by a single event; it accumulates silently through small inconsistencies, delayed reconciliations, and overlooked obligations. AI monitors risk continuously. It identifies exposure early, whether related to tax liability, cash flow volatility, payroll compliance, or reporting gaps. This allows businesses to respond proactively rather than defensively.

AI also enables scenario planning at a level traditional systems cannot match. By modeling how regulatory changes, economic shifts, or operational decisions affect financial outcomes, AI allows leaders to prepare multiple futures instead of reacting to one. This foresight transforms uncertainty into strategy. Businesses stop guessing what might happen and start planning for what could.

Perhaps most importantly, AI accounting future-proofs leadership itself. Leaders who trust their financial systems operate differently. They are less reactive. They make long-term investments. They build with resilience rather than urgency. AI creates the conditions for sustainable decision-making by ensuring that financial truth remains stable even as external conditions change.

In an era where compliance is continuous, audits are automated, and transparency is unavoidable, future-proofing is not optional. AI accounting systems do not promise certainty—but they provide preparedness. And in the modern financial landscape, preparedness is power.

"The Audit That Never Came"

Marcus used to believe that success invited attention. The bigger his company became, the more he expected someone to come knocking—an auditor, a regulator, a lender with impossible questions. For years, that expectation shaped how he experienced growth. Every expansion came with excitement and unease in equal measure. He built carefully, but he never felt safe.

Marcus's company operated in a heavily regulated industry. Multiple states. Multiple filings. Constant updates to reporting rules. Early on, he had learned the hard way that compliance mistakes were rarely forgiven. A missed filing years earlier had cost him penalties and sleepless nights. Since then, he lived with a quiet belief that another reckoning was inevitable.

The shift to AI accounting happened gradually. At first, Marcus adopted it for efficiency. Then for accuracy. Over time, something deeper changed. The system didn't just record transactions—it watched patterns. It flagged risks before they matured. It adjusted workflows when regulations changed. It asked questions Marcus hadn't thought to ask.

Years passed. The company grew. Revenue increased. Complexity multiplied. Marcus waited for the moment when something would break.

It never did.

One year, a competitor was audited aggressively. Another was fined for reporting inconsistencies. Industry news buzzed with enforcement actions and compliance failures. Marcus braced himself. He reviewed reports. He checked documentation. Everything aligned. The numbers told one clear story.

Months went by. No letters. No notices. No inquiries.

Marcus realized something unsettling and comforting at the same time: the absence of crisis was not luck. It was design.

The AI system had quietly future-proofed the company. It had adapted as rules changed. It had preserved records in formats that held up over time. It had reduced risk without drama. Marcus hadn't noticed because nothing had gone wrong.

One evening, Marcus reviewed a multi-year financial archive. Every year aligned. Every report reconciled. Every filing matched the books. The story was complete and defensible.

He closed his laptop and leaned back. For the first time, he understood that the goal was never to avoid attention—it was to be ready for it. And readiness, he realized, was the quietest form of success.

The audit never came. And for Marcus, that silence was the loudest confirmation of all.

Chapter 10

The Invisible CFO: How AI Becomes the Most Reliable Financial Leader in the Business

The highest level of bookkeeping and accounting is not accuracy alone, but stewardship. At maturity, financial systems do more than record transactions, enforce compliance, or generate reports—they guide the business. They quietly protect it from mistakes, alert it to opportunities, and ensure that decisions are grounded in truth rather than assumption. Artificial intelligence reaches this level by functioning as an invisible chief financial officer, operating continuously in the background, never distracted, never biased, and never fatigued. This is the culmination of AI bookkeeping: not software that assists finance teams, but intelligence that embodies financial leadership itself.

Traditional CFO functions depend heavily on experience, intuition, and selective information. Even the best human financial leaders must rely on summaries, reports, and interpretations that arrive after events have already occurred. AI operates differently. It does not wait for reports—it observes reality as it unfolds. It tracks every dollar, every obligation, every pattern, and every deviation simultaneously. This omnipresent awareness allows AI to detect risks and opportunities at a speed no human can match. The result is financial governance that is proactive rather than reactive.

AI's role as an invisible CFO is most evident in decision support. Every major business decision—hiring, expansion, investment, pricing, restructuring—has financial consequences. AI models these consequences instantly. It shows how a decision will affect cash flow, profitability, tax exposure, and compliance before the decision is finalized. This transforms leadership. Decisions are no longer made in isolation or corrected later; they are evaluated holistically from the start.

AI also enforces discipline without emotion. Human leadership is vulnerable to optimism, pressure, and fatigue. AI applies the same standards consistently, regardless of circumstance. It does not loosen controls during periods of success or panic during downturns. This stability is critical for long-term sustainability. Businesses guided by AI maintain financial integrity through growth cycles, market shifts, and leadership changes.

Another defining trait of the invisible CFO is institutional memory. Human teams change. Knowledge is lost. Practices drift. AI preserves financial logic across time. It remembers how transactions were classified, how policies were applied, and how risks were mitigated. This continuity protects the business from regression and ensures that financial excellence is not dependent on individual people.

AI also strengthens external credibility. Investors, lenders, regulators, and partners trust businesses that present clear, consistent, and defensible financial records. AI delivers this trust automatically. Financial narratives are aligned. Documentation is complete. Reports are reliable. The business speaks with one financial voice.

Ultimately, the invisible CFO is not about replacing humans—it is about elevating them. When AI handles vigilance, verification, and analysis, leaders are free to focus on vision, strategy, and execution. Accounting becomes silent, stable, and strong.

This is the final evolution of bookkeeping. Not chaos managed. Not compliance enforced. But stewardship embedded. AI becomes the financial conscience of the business—always watching, always guiding, always prepared.

"The Business That Never Panicked Again"

No one noticed the moment it happened, which was fitting, because nothing dramatic occurred.

There was no crisis. No emergency meeting. No urgent call from finance. Just a quiet shift in how the business felt.

For nearly a decade, Thomas had lived with tension. Not visible tension—he smiled in meetings, approved budgets, signed contracts—but a constant undercurrent of unease. His company was successful by every external measure. Revenue grew steadily. Clients stayed loyal. Employees respected him. Yet every major decision carried weight. Every expansion raised questions. Every tax season brought unease.

Thomas had learned early in his career that financial problems rarely announced themselves loudly. They crept in quietly, disguised as timing issues, minor discrepancies, or assumptions no one questioned. He had seen companies fail not because they lacked talent or vision, but because their financial foundations cracked under pressure.

The transition to AI bookkeeping happened gradually, almost reluctantly. Thomas didn't adopt it to transform the business—he adopted it to reduce stress. He wanted fewer surprises. Fewer late nights. Fewer moments of doubt.

At first, the AI system felt like a highly competent assistant. It organized data. It reconciled accounts. It flagged inconsistencies. Over time, it became something else entirely. It anticipated questions before they were asked. It modeled outcomes before decisions were finalized. It surfaced risks while they were still theoretical.

Then came the year that tested everything.

A sudden market shift disrupted several competitors. Supply chains tightened. Costs rose unpredictably. Rumors of layoffs spread across the industry. Boards panicked. Executives reacted emotionally. Thomas watched carefully, waiting for the same pressure to hit his company.

It didn't.

When costs rose, the AI adjusted forecasts immediately. When revenue slowed in one segment, it highlighted stronger areas. When tax exposure shifted, reserves were already in place. There was no scramble, no confusion, no panic. Meetings remained calm. Decisions remained measured.

Employees noticed. Managers noticed. The business didn't feel immune—but it felt prepared.

Late one evening, Thomas reviewed a dashboard showing years of financial history aligned perfectly. No gaps. No contradictions. No unexplained adjustments. The numbers told a clear story—not just of success, but of resilience.

That was when Thomas understood what had changed.

The business no longer depended on constant vigilance from exhausted humans. It no longer relied on hope that things would work out. It had a financial guardian—one that never slept, never guessed, and never forgot.

The company didn't panic anymore because it didn't have to.

Thomas closed his laptop and turned off the lights. For the first time in his career, success felt stable. Not fragile. Not temporary.

And in that quiet certainty, he realized that the greatest leadership decision he had ever made was choosing a system that could lead financially even when no one was watching.

Final Thoughts

Perfect financial documentation has always been treated as an ideal rather than a reality. Businesses hoped their records were good enough, their reports accurate enough, their documentation complete enough to survive tax season, lender scrutiny, or regulatory review. For decades, "good enough" was the best most organizations could achieve because the systems themselves were fragile. They depended on memory, manual input, delayed reconciliation, and human interpretation layered on top of fragmented data. Artificial intelligence ends that era. It replaces approximation with precision and transforms financial documentation from a recurring risk into a permanent asset.

Throughout this book, one truth has become increasingly clear: bookkeeping is not merely an administrative task. It is the language through which a business explains itself to the world. Financial records tell the story of how money moves, how decisions are made, how risk is managed, and how responsibility is upheld. When that story is incomplete or inconsistent, the business appears unreliable—even when it is honest. AI corrects this not by forcing perfection through effort, but by designing perfection into the system itself. Documentation is no longer something businesses chase; it is something they generate automatically as they operate.

What makes AI bookkeeping transformative is not just automation, but continuity. Human systems work in bursts—monthly closes, quarterly reviews, annual filings. AI works continuously. It does not forget transactions, overlook receipts, or delay reconciliation. It builds financial truth minute by minute, creating a record that is always current and always defensible. This continuity eliminates the stress cycles that have historically defined accounting. There is no buildup to panic, no scramble to reconstruct history, no uncertainty about whether the numbers will hold up under scrutiny. The work is already done.

This shift fundamentally changes the relationship between businesses and compliance. Compliance has long been treated as an external pressure imposed by tax authorities and regulators. AI reframes compliance as an internal state of readiness. When records are complete, categorized correctly, and verified in real time, compliance stops being reactive. Filing becomes procedural. Audits become manageable. Reporting becomes routine. The fear that once surrounded these events dissolves because the underlying data is solid.

Equally important is the strategic clarity that emerges when documentation is perfect. Clean records reveal patterns that messy systems obscure. They show where money is truly made, where it is wasted, where margins erode, and where opportunities hide. This clarity empowers leaders to act decisively rather than cautiously. Growth becomes intentional instead of risky. Investment decisions are informed instead of speculative. AI bookkeeping does not just protect the past—it informs the future.

Another lasting impact of AI-driven documentation is institutional resilience. Businesses change. Teams turn over. Processes evolve. Knowledge is lost. Traditional systems degrade over time as consistency erodes and shortcuts accumulate. AI preserves financial logic across years, ensuring that documentation remains stable even as people and operations change. This continuity is invaluable. It protects businesses from regression and ensures that financial excellence does not depend on specific individuals.

AI also reshapes the role of human expertise. Accountants, tax professionals, and financial advisors are no longer consumed by cleanup and correction. With clean records as a foundation, they move into higher-value roles focused on optimization, strategy, and long-term planning. This elevates the entire financial ecosystem surrounding the business. Conversations become proactive rather than corrective. Advice becomes strategic rather than defensive.

Perhaps the most profound outcome of AI bookkeeping is psychological. Business owners who trust their records operate differently. They sleep better. They plan further ahead. They stop second-guessing decisions made months earlier. Financial confidence becomes part of leadership identity rather than something borrowed from external validation. This internal shift is subtle but powerful. It changes how businesses grow, how they respond to challenges, and how they define success.

As financial oversight becomes increasingly digital and data-driven, the margin for error will continue to shrink. Tax authorities, lenders, and regulators are no longer limited by human review cycles. They use automated tools to detect inconsistencies, anomalies, and patterns across massive datasets. Businesses that rely on outdated bookkeeping methods will find themselves increasingly exposed—not because they are dishonest, but because their documentation cannot withstand modern scrutiny. AI bookkeeping is not a future advantage; it is a present requirement.

This book has shown that perfect financial documentation is no longer aspirational. It is achievable. It is scalable. And it is sustainable. AI does not promise to eliminate responsibility or replace judgment. Instead, it creates a system where responsibility is supported, judgment is informed, and documentation is reliable by design.

The future of business finance belongs to those who build systems that are always ready, always accurate, and always aligned with reality. AI bookkeeping is not about doing accounting faster—it is about doing it correctly, continuously, and confidently. When financial truth is stable, everything else becomes easier: compliance, growth, strategy, and leadership itself.

In closing, the ultimate value of AI bookkeeping is not found in software features or technical specifications. It is found in the quiet absence of chaos. In the smooth tax season. In the calm audit. In the confident decision. In the business that no longer worries about being exposed because it knows its records are right.

That is what perfect financial documentation looks like in practice. And that is what artificial intelligence finally makes possible.

www.ingramcontent.com/pod-product-compliance
Ingram Content Group UK Ltd.
Pitfield, Milton Keynes, MK11 3LW, UK
UKHW020155290926
15471UKWH00005B/882

9 798295 593352